A HOR █████████████ C

D1125219

# HORRID HENRY'S
# FOOD

to Ishani
Love Kresh 2014

**Francesca Simon** spent her
childhood on the beach in California, and
then went to Yale and Oxford universities
to study medieval history and literature.
She now lives in London with her family.
She has written over fifty books, and won the
Children's Book of the Year in 2008 at the
Galaxy British Book Awards for *Horrid Henry
and the Abominable Snowman*.


**Tony Ross** is one of Britain's
best-known illustrators, with many
picture books to his name as well as
line drawings for many fiction titles.
He lives in Oxfordshire.

Complete list of **Horrid Henry** titles
at the end of the book

Also by Francesca Simon

*Don't Cook Cinderella*
*Helping Hercules*

and for younger readers

*Don't Be Horrid, Henry*
Illustrated by Kevin McAleenan

*The Parent Swap Shop*
Illustrated by Pete Williamson

*Spider School*
Illustrated by Tony Ross

*The Topsy-Turvies*
Illustrated by Emily Bolam

# A HORRID FACTBOOK

# HORRID HENRY'S FOOD

## Francesca Simon

Illustrated by Tony Ross

Orion
Children's Books

First published in Great Britain in 2012
by Orion Children's Books
a division of the Orion Publishing Group Ltd
Orion House
5 Upper Saint Martin's Lane
London WC2H 9EA
An Hachette UK Company

1 3 5 7 9 10 8 6 4 2

Facts compiled by Sally Byford.

The Orion Publishing Group's policy is to use papers
that are natural, renewable and recyclable products and
made from wood grown in sustainable forests. The logging
and manufacturing processes are expected to conform to
the environmental regulations of the country of origin.

ISBN 978 1 4440 0633 9

A catalogue record for this book
is available from the British Library.

Printed in Great Britain by
Clays Ltd, St Ives plc

www.orionbooks.co.uk
www.horridhenry.co.uk

# CONTENTS

Clever Clare's First Facts                    1

Insider Info                                  5

Perfect Peter's Fab Fruit and Virtuous Veg    9

Fast Food – Yeah!                            19

Foods Around the World                       25

Weird Restaurants                            33

Mad Myths                                    39

Champion Chocolate                           45

Crunchy Creepy-Crawlies                      51

Mystery Meals                                57

Biggest, Longest, Hottest, Smelliest . . .   63

Scary Snacks                                 71

Blecccch! Gross Grub                         77

Posh Nosh and Festive Feasts                 83

Strange but True                             93

# Hello from Henry

**Hey gang!**

**Food! Yummy yummy food! Who wouldn't want to know more about burgers and chips and pizza, ice cream and chocolate and sweets and . . . what's this? There's info on . . . veg? And fruit? What?**

**This is MY food factbook. No one wants to know about how many sprouts sad people eat every year, or why apples float.**

Actually it's fun to KNOW that stuff, as long as you don't have to eat them. The world's biggest cupcake? Now we're talking!

Happy reading!

Henry

# CLEVER CLARE'S FIRST FACTS

Most of the food we eat is either from **animals** – for example, meat, eggs and cheese – or plants – **fruit** and **vegetables**.

Food gives us **energy**, and the amount of energy in food is measured in **calories**. The more energetic we are, the more calories we burn.

An average person eats about one kilogram of food a day, which is the weight of a litre bottle of water ...

... which means you eat **365 kilograms** of food in a year – the same weight as a **fully grown bull** ...

If food **smells good**, it **tastes good** too, because 90% of the taste comes from the smell.

If we are ill or injured, food gives us the goodness we need to heal our bodies and get better.

By the time you are 70 years old, you'll have eaten 25,500 kilograms, or 25.5 tonnes – and that's **the same as six elephants!**

Our own **senses** play a big part in the kind of food we like too.

If a plate of food looks nice and it's something you've eaten before, you think it looks tastier than a plate of **strangely shaped** and **coloured** food.

Your brain tells you to like **burgers**, **chips**, **cakes** and **sweets** because it knows that these foods are full of sugar and fat and provide you with lots of energy. No wonder Horrid Henry likes fast food more than salad and vegetables!

# INSIDER INFO

As soon as you smell tasty food, like **chips** or **pizza**, your mouth gets ready to eat by producing lots of spit.

When you bite into your food, your teeth and spit start to break it down . . . then it takes just **seven seconds** to travel from your mouth to your tummy down a long stretchy pipe called the **oesophagus**.

The oesophagus has powerful muscles which move in waves to **squeeze your food** down.

Your stomach **mashes up the food**, and it continues its journey down a six-metre tube called the small intestine.

In your stomach, there are **powerful acids** which break down the food.

After about **12 hours**, your food is fully digested. The nutrients, or good bits, travel via your liver to your blood to help your body **grow** and **stay healthy**.

The leftover bits travel to the large intestine, which is shorter than the small intestine but twice as wide. The watery leftovers leave your body as **wee**, and the solid leftovers as **poo**.

If you throw up your food, **your vomit** will probably look like **carrots!** Vomit nearly always looks like carrots, whatever you've eaten, because the orange stuff is part of your **stomach lining**.

**Ewww!**

**Apples** and **sprouts** make Horrid Henry feel sick, but his mum tries to make him eat them because fruit and vegetables are very good for you.

# PERFECT PETER'S FAB FRUIT AND VIRTUOUS VEG

People who choose not to eat meat and fish are called **vegetarians**.

People who don't eat or use any products made from animals – including eggs, milk, honey and leather – are called **vegans**.

Whether you're an omnivore (eating everything), a vegetarian or a vegan, it's good for you to have five servings of **fab fruit** and **virtuous veggies** a day.

Did you know that **tomatoes** and **cucumbers** aren't really vegetables? They are fruit, because they both contain the seeds of the plant.

**Tomatoes** are the **most popular fruit** worldwide – with more than 60 million tonnes produced every year. **Bananas** are the second favourite – with 44 million tonnes produced a year, followed by **apples**, **oranges** and **watermelons**.

Did you know that the reason apples **float in water** is because they are made of 25% air.

**Strawberries** are the only fruit with seeds on the outside skin.

Can you believe it? **Lemons** contain more sugar than **strawberries**.

When you eat a **baked potato**, it's best to eat the skin because that's where the goodness is.

Until the Seventeenth Century, all carrots used to be **purple!** Sometimes the purple carrots were discoloured with yellow streaks, and when growers realised that these ones tasted sweeter, they gradually developed them into the **orange variety** we have today.

For Christmas, **15,000 tonnes of sprouts** are bought in the UK, with **each person eating around 15**.

**Count me out! Peter can have mine**.

When you cut an onion, it releases a gas which irritates your eyes. Your eyes release water to wash the gas away – that's why onions make you cry.

**Broccoli** is a vegetable, but it's also a flower.

If you like liquorice, you might like a vegetable called **fennel** which has a similar flavour.

A grapefruit crossed with a mandarin produces such an unattractive fruit, with a baggy, lumpy skin, that it's called the **ugli fruit**.

Not all fruit smells nice. The **durian** is a
**big, spiny fruit** from South-East Asia – it
tastes sweet, but people say it smells like
sweaty socks.

**I'd call it the Margaret.**

The Japanese have created **square
watermelons**, by growing them in a
square glass box, so that they fit neatly
into the fridge.

The largest fruits are giant **pumpkins**, sometimes weighing over 450 kilograms – that's **as heavy as a cow!**

**Avocados** are also called 'alligator pears' because they are the shape of a pear with a rough, green skin like an alligator.

Boost your brainpower for an exam by eating **blueberries**, **tomatoes**, **blackcurrants** or **broccoli**. They are all supposed to help memory and quick thinking.

**Wow! No one thinks faster than me. If I started eating blueberries, tomatoes, blackcurrants or broccoli, I could . . . I would . . . Naah!**

# FAST FOOD – YEAH!

The **first fast food restaurant** opened in 1912 in New York, USA. It was called Automat and its slogan was 'Less Work for Mother'. It wasn't like today's fast food – it included **macaroni cheese**, **steak and mashed potatoes**, and **rice pudding**.

**Drive-through** fast food restaurants were also started in America in the 1930s, and have grown in popularity as more people have cars.

Horrid Henry loves the bright lights and loud music in his favourite restaurant, **Gobble and Go**. Fast food restaurants are specially designed like this to make people eat quickly and leave, to make room for the next customers!

Britons eat **seven million pounds** worth of fast food every day, including more than **600,000 pizzas** a year.

But the most famous fast food in the UK is **fish and chips**.

**Pizza** was first made in **Italy** – it started as a sort of tomato pie and then cheese was added in 1889. As Italians moved to other countries, pizza became one of the **most popular foods** around the world.

Now over **five billion pizzas** are sold worldwide each year.

**And I eat most of them!**

According to one pizza take-away company, most people order pizza during the TV weather forecast.

The reason burgers are often called **'hamburgers'** even though they are made of beef, is because they were first made in **Hamburg in Germany**.

On average there are **180 sesame seeds** on a burger bun.

Drive-through burger bars are everywhere now, but in Sälen in Sweden, they've opened something completely new – the world's first **ski-through burger bar**. Now that really is fast food!

In Oak Brook, Illinois, you can study fast food at the **Hamburger University**. So far, over **50,000 students** from all over the world have graduated with degrees in **Hamburgerology**.

**Let's make that 50,001.**

To grow the potatoes needed for a year's supply of chips in the UK takes an area the size of **45,000 football pitches** ...

... and if you laid all these potatoes end-to-end, they would stretch around the world **76 times**. That's a lot of chips!

**Yum!**

# FOODS
# AROUND
# THE WORLD

Horrid Henry's favourite foods are **pizza**, **burgers**, **crisps**, **chips** and **chocolate**. Around the world, people like all sorts of different foods.

The **USA** is well-known for its **apple pies**, which is why we say 'as American as apple pie'. In the Nineteenth Century, Americans even ate apple pie for breakfast.

In **Australia**, you can eat **crocodile sausages** and **kangaroo meat**.

The Aborigines of **Australia** eat **kangaroo**, **turkey** and **goanna**, a type of **lizard**. They call their food 'bush-tucks'.

The **French** are famous for **cheese** – and make more than **350** different kinds. The average French person eats about 65 grams of cheese a day, compared to 30 grams for a British person.

**Feijoada**, a stew of black beans, pork and spices, is a popular dish in **Brazil**. If you try it, watch out – it sometimes contains **pigs' feet** and **ears**.

**Dim sum** is a **Chinese** dish of bite-sized portions of noodles, dumplings, vegetables and meat.

Favourite meals in **Great Britain** include **fish and chips** and **roast beef and Yorkshire pudding**, but one of the most popular dishes is a curry – **chicken tikka masala**.

There are around **11,000 fish and chip shops** in **Great Britain**, and in one year the British consume 300 million servings of fish and chips, which is six servings each for every person.

**Moussaka** – a casserole made of lamb, aubergine, tomatoes and spices – is **Greece's** best-known meal.

In **Iceland**, people eat **hákarl**, a meal made of **shark** meat.

**Samosas** are popular **Indian** snacks or starters, made of meat, potatoes, vegetables and spices stuffed inside paástry dough and fried in oil.

In **Ireland**, the best-known dish is **Irish stew** – a filling meal of mutton, potatoes and onions.

The **Japanese** are well-known for their **sushi** – bite-sized pieces of cooked rice topped with raw fish and wrapped in seaweed.

**India** is known for its **curries**, and after the British introduced curry to **Japan** in the Nineteenth Century, it's one of the most popular dishes there too, with Japanese people eating it around 62 times a year.

**Ceviche** is a traditional dish in **Mexico** — raw fish soaked in lemon juice, with onions, tomatoes and herbs. The acid in the lemon juice cooks the fish, without using any heat.

**Haggis** is a famous food from **Scotland**. It's made from offal, suet, onions and oatmeal, all stuffed into a sheep's stomach.

**That's not food, that's torture.**

In **South Africa**, people love **bobotie** – a dish made of minced lamb or beef, bread, rice or potatoes, onions and spices, mixed with egg and milk, then baked.

**Paella** is a popular **Spanish** rice dish, which can contain chicken, vegetables, meat or seafood.

**Pad Thai** – rice noodles stir-fried with peanuts, oil, vegetables and chicken – is **Thailand's** most popular dish.

The national dish of **Wales** is called **cawl**, a hearty stew made from bacon, lamb or beef, cabbage and leeks. The gravy is sometimes eaten first, like soup, followed by the meat and vegetables as a main course.

# WEIRD RESTAURANTS

Horrid Henry's favourite restaurant is
**Gobble and Go**, and he's even eaten snails at
**Restaurant Le Posh**. But he'd be amazed by
some of these really weird restaurants . . .

The **Redwoods Treehouse** in New Zealand
is a pod-shaped restaurant built ten metres
above ground, around a giant redwood tree
trunk. Diners reach the restaurant along a
treetop walkway.

Ithaa Undersea Restaurant in the Maldives
is the world's first **all-glass**, **undersea**
eatery. It's five metres below sea level, so
you get a great view of all the **sea life**
while you eat.

You can dine **45 metres above the ground**
in Belgium, in the **Sky Restaurant** which
dangles from a crane. Luckily, diners are
strapped to their seats!

The **Modern Toilet** is a chain of restaurants across Hong Kong and Taiwan. The seats are toilets (but they don't flush!) and the food is served in **toilet-shaped bowls**.

There is a **robotic restaurant** in Germany. Actually, there aren't any robots, but there aren't any waiters either. You order your food via touch screen and it **whizzes to your table on rails**. The cooks are real people though!

The creepy **Vampire Café** in Tokyo, Japan, has **blood red walls** decorated with **skulls** and waiters dressed like **vampires** from a horror movie.

In a London restaurant called **Dans Le Noir** (which means 'in the dark') guests eat in the **pitch dark**. The idea is that because you can't see the food, you concentrate only on the taste.

You don't need a ticket to eat at the **A380 In-Flight Kitchen** in Taiwan. Named after the giant Airbus airliner, it's a restaurant that looks exactly like **the inside of a plane**, complete with baggage compartments and waitresses dressed as flight attendants.

In Toyko, most people have small homes with no room for pets. But at the **Calico Cat Café**, they can rent a cat to stroke while they eat.

# MAD
# MYTHS

**Eating crusts doesn't** make your hair curly. It's a food fib your parents use to make you eat up all your sandwich!

Eating lots of **carrots** could make **your skin look orange**. This is because they are full of something called 'carotene', the orange pigment that makes the carrots orange.

**Or you could just have a carrot nose like Miss Battle-Axe.**

Carrots are also full of **Vitamin A**, which really does help you see better **in the dark**. But carrots only help if you are short of Vitamin A in the first place, so it is a bit of a myth.

**Chewing gum** doesn't take any longer than other foods to digest. In fact, it comes out of you looking the same as when it went in!

**Dropped toast** doesn't always land buttered side down. Even though, when you're hungry, it probably seems as if it does.

Lots of jokes involve people slipping on **banana skins**, but actually, banana skins don't always make people slip. It's only the **slimy old skins** that do!

Brown eggs **aren't** necessarily healthier than white eggs. It's just that different types of hens have different eggshell colours.

Despite what people think, **chocolate doesn't give you spots**. But the milk in milk chocolate might.

Lobsters don't really **scream** when you boil them – they don't have vocal chords, so they can't make any noise. The screaming sound is the **steam escaping** from their shells.

The ancient Egyptians believed that onions kept evil spirits at bay, so when they made a promise, they placed **one hand on an onion**.

**Throwing rice** at weddings was believed to be **good luck** for the wedding couple, because rice symbolised health and wealth.

In Hungary, people moving into a new house **throw salt** near the doorway to protect their home from **evil**.

# CHAMPION
# CHOCOLATE

In the UK, we eat **£4.3 billion** worth of chocolate a year . . .

. . . which is about **11 kilograms** each, the same weight as 11 bags of sugar!

The word **chocolate** comes from the Mexican word **xocolatl**, which means bitter water.

In the Sixteenth Century, a Spanish explorer brought chocolate from Mexico to King Charles V of Spain in the form of **cocoa beans**. Chocolate was soon popular in Spain as a hot chocolate drink.

The first chocolate house, or café, was opened in the UK in London in 1657.

Over 1,400 years ago, the Mayan and Aztec people in Mexico used **cocoa beans as money**. A large tomato was worth one cocoa bean, a rabbit ten beans, and **a slave was worth a hundred beans**.

**Chocolate cheers us up!** As well as tasting yummy, it releases **endorphins** in our brains, which makes us **feel happy**.

Eating one small square of dark chocolate a day is good for your heart. It contains **flavanols** that help to keep your blood pumping happily around your body.

The **first** chocolate **Easter egg** was produced in 1873 by Fry's.

In 2006, the most expensive Easter egg ever was created – the **Diamond Stella Easter Egg**, laden with diamonds, which cost **£50,000!**

The average chocolate bar contains **eight insect legs**, which have fallen in accidentally.

Chocolate is **poisonous to dogs**. Some of the chemicals in chocolate can make a dog's heart race so fast that it could have a seizure. The smaller the dog, the more dangerous it is to give it chocolate.

In a famous old horror film called 'Psycho', **chocolate syrup** was used as fake blood.

Did you know you can buy **meat-flavoured** chocolate? It's made from dark chocolate and ground-up salty dried meat.

Other weird and wonderful flavours of chocolate include **pepper**, **chilli**, **cauliflower**, and **basil and tomato**.

# CRUNCHY
# CREEPY-
# CRAWLIES

The number of people in the world is growing very quickly and it's getting harder to find enough meat and fish for everyone to eat. So – yum yum – insects are the food of the future! **Ants**, **crickets** and **locusts** are easy to farm and have much less fat than meat.

Already, **1,000 species of insects** are eaten around the world, in eighty per cent of countries.

The most popular insects to eat worldwide are **beetles** and **cockroaches**, followed by **flies** and **lice**.

Eating insects isn't a new idea. In 1995, Vincent M Holt wrote a book called 'Why Not Eat Insects?' He had lots of delicious recipe ideas, like **slug soup**, **snail sauce**, **moths in butter** and **braised beef with caterpillars**.

The colouring in pink icing and pink marshmallow is made from **grinding down ants**.

In Japan and China, **grasshoppers** are fried and served with rice.

**Sun-dried maggots** are another favourite food in China.

On the shelves of Mexican supermarkets, you'll find cans of **caterpillars**.

In Cambodia, a popular snack is deep-fried
big black hairy **spiders** the size of your palm!
They taste a bit like chicken or fish.

In Australia, you can eat **witchety grubs**,
which are actually moth larvae, about the size
of your small finger, and they can be eaten
raw or baked.

Scientists have suggested that even if we don't think we're eating creepy-crawlies, so many bug bits fall into our food accidentally that we all eat about **500 grams of insects every year**.

**Eeeeeeew!**

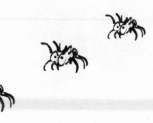

# MYSTERY
# MEALS

Have you ever eaten **venison and veal** and wondered what they are? These mystery meats are actually **deer and calf**.

**Guacamole** is a Mexican dip made from **mashed avocados**.

**Beefsteak** sounds like meat, but it's really a type of tomato.

A **truffle** is an edible fungi that grows underground and is snuffled out by pigs.

**Buffalo wings** have nothing to do with buffalos! They are spicy chicken wings that were invented in Buffalo, New York.

**Hummus** is a Middle Eastern dish made from mashed chickpeas.

**Spam** is SPiced hAM in a tin, and is more popular in Hawaii than anywhere else in the world.

**Steak tartare** is completely raw beef minced up with onions, egg and seasoning.

**Bubble and squeak** is a meal made from left-over vegetables, fried until it's brown, and it gets its name from the sound it makes when it's cooking in the pan.

**Black pudding** looks like a black sausage, and it's made from **dried pig's blood and fat**.

**Toad-in-the-hole** is really sausages baked in batter.

**Mulligatawny soup** is a curry-flavoured soup, created in India in the Eighteenth Century for serving to the British.

**Stargazey Pie** is a pie made in Cornwall from pilchards, herring or mackerel. The pie gets its name because the fish heads are left outside the pastry gazing up to the sky.

# BIGGEST, LONGEST, HOTTEST, SMELLIEST...

**Biggest cupcake –** made in the USA in 2009, it had a circumference of 3.5 metres. It was made from 90 kilograms of flour, 90 kilograms of sugar, 90 kilograms of butter and 800 eggs, and took 12 hours to bake. At 1.2 metres tall, this cupcake was as tall as an average seven year old.

**Biggest pie –** a pumpkin pie baked in 2010 in Ohio, USA, weighing 1,680 kilograms, and six metres wide – that's three tall men laid end to end. The ingredients were 550 kilograms of canned pumpkin, 2,796 eggs, 109 gallons of evaporated milk, 238 kilograms of sugar, 3 kilograms of salt and 7 kilograms of cinnamon.

**Biggest pizza –** made in December 1990 in South Africa, it measured an incredible 37.4 metres wide – more than two buses end to end – and included 500 kilograms of flour, 800 kilograms of cheese and 900 kilograms of tomato paste.

**Biggest custard-pie fight –** in 2000, 20 people at the Millennium Dome in London threw 3,312 custard pies in three minutes.

**Longest bean –** in 1997, American Harry Hurley grew a bean that measured 1.3 metres, the height of an average eight-year-old boy.

**Longest sandwich –** created in Italy in 2004 from a 634 metre-long loaf. The sandwich contained 550 kilograms of salami and cheese, and was big enough to feed 19,000 people.

**Longest cucumber –** grown by Clare Pearce in the UK in August 2010, it measured 1.2 metres, about the height of an average seven year old.

**Longest carrot –** grown by Joe Atherton in the UK in 2007, it measured an amazing 5.8 metres long, the same length as a crocodile.

**Hottest curry –** the Naga Madras curry which contains the fiercely hot **Naga Viper** chilli. Only two people have ever managed to finish a whole plateful!

**Smelliest cheese** – scientists at a UK university have discovered the smelliest cheese using an electronic nose. It's a soft cheese from France called **Vieux Boulogne**. It's even stinkier than a cheese called Epoisses de Bourgogne, which is **so pongy** it's been **banned from public transport**.

**Most expensive pizza –** a Valentine's Day pizza made in the USA worth £1,700. Its toppings included venison, lobster and **edible gold**.

**Largest Easter egg –** made by the Belgian chocolate producer Guylian, the egg measured 8.32 metres high – taller than a house. It took 26 craftsmen 525 hours to make the egg, using 1,950 kilograms of chocolate – about 50,000 bars of chocolate.

**Oldest soup –** archaeologists have discovered that people ate soup as long ago as **6000 BC** – it was **hippopotamus soup**.

# SCARY
# SNACKS

Around 70 million people all around the world suffer from **food poisoning** every year – and about seven million of them actually die.

**Be careful!** Raw chicken or eggs could contain a bacteria called **salmonella** which can make you ill. So think twice before licking the spoon after making a cake or cooking chicken.

A **mouldy sandwich** is full of **bacteria** and covered in poisonous green fungi, so if you take a bite by mistake it'll make you very sick.

Some Japanese people like to dice with death by eating a **poisonous fish called fugu**. The poison is in the fugu's eyeballs and liver, so if those parts are properly removed, there's no danger. But if they aren't – **you're dead!**

The person cooking the fugu has to be an expert chef and has to taste the fugu first. But even though the expert chefs are very careful, fugu still kills about **300 people a year**.

Around 8% of children and 2% of adults have **a food allergy**, which means their bodies decide a certain food is dangerous and attack it.

The most common foods that people are allergic to are tree nuts – like walnuts and cashews – peanuts, milk, eggs, soy, wheat, fish and shellfish.

**Casu marzu**, meaning **'rotten cheese'** is a truly revolting Italian cheese. When it's made, flies are added to it, so that by the time the cheese is ready to eat, it's full of **plump grubs** which jump off the cheese while you're eating it. If you tempted to try this **scary snack**, be warned – it can make you very ill indeed. But some people still think it's delicious.

Luckily, **your senses** of taste and smell usually warn you off **mouldy or poisonous food**. If you do put something horrible in your mouth, you spit it out – which stops it getting into your stomach and making you ill.

# BLECCCCH! GROSS GRUB

When blue cheese, like **blue Stilton** or **Gorgonzola**, is being made, a mould called **Penicillium** is added to it. When the cheese is ready to eat, it's spotted with blue mould and really smelly.

**Yogurt** is really **gone-off milk!** The milk is 'curdled' by adding bacteria, which gives yogurt its tangy taste.

**Bird's nest soup** is an Asian speciality made from the hardened spit that swifts use to build their nests.

You really can eat a **cow's tongue** – the meat is lean, boneless and full of protein.

Have you ever tried **offal?** It includes hearts, lungs, livers, and kidneys, plus the delicious-sounding sweetbreads, which are actually cow glands.

If anyone offers you **brawn**, beware. It's jellied pig's head and it looks like jelly full of bits of chewed-up meat.

**Black pudding** looks like a sausage, but it's made of **blood**.

In Korea, **baby octopus** is served and swallowed whole, still *alive and wriggling!*

In Alaska, **salmon heads** are buried in the ground and left for a few weeks, before being mashed and eaten. Not surprisingly, this dish is nicknamed **'stink heads'**.

In Taiwan, a cake made of rice and **pig's blood** is sold on wooden sticks and eaten like ice cream.

That harmless little bottle of Worcestershire sauce in your fridge is made from salty little fish called **anchovies** – bones and all – dissolved in vinegar.

**Jellied blood** is eaten in China. It looks like jelly, but it's made out of duck's or pig's blood!

In Japan, you could try **shiokara** – fresh raw fish served in a sauce made of fermented **fish or squid guts**.

If you've ever tucked into the traditional British dish, **tripe and onions**, you've eaten the lining of a **cow's stomach**.

**Jellied eels** are a favourite old London dish sold from street stalls and sprinkled with hot chilli vinegar.

# POSH NOSH
## AND
# FESTIVE
# FEASTS

The largest dish ever is the **roast camel**, a favourite at wedding feasts in the Middle East. A fish is stuffed with eggs, the fish is stuffed inside a chicken, the chicken is stuffed inside a sheep, and the sheep is stuffed inside the camel and roasted.

**Sandwiches** were named after the Fourth Earl of Sandwich. He didn't want to leave the gambling table to eat, so his servant gave him beef between two slices of bread.

At Elizabethan feasts, they really did eat **'four and twenty blackbirds baked in a pie'**. But the birds weren't really baked – the crust was cooked and then laid over the birds. When the crust was broken, the birds flew out.

**Peach Melba** – a pudding combining **ice cream**, **peaches** and **raspberry sauce** – was invented at a hotel in the late Nineteenth Century to celebrate the Australian opera singer, **Nellie Melba**. The pudding was presented to Dame Melba in an ice sculpture of a swan.

On New Year's Eve, in Madrid, Spain, people count down the last minutes of the old year by popping **grapes** into their mouths.

In Japan, the New Year's food is a fish called **red snapper**, which is considered **lucky** because of its colour.

In Greece, a cake called **peta** is baked with a **coin inside**. It's thought that the person who gets the slice with the coin will have **special luck** in the coming year.

In Tibet, Buddhists celebrate the New Year with a dish called **guthok**, which contains a piece of charcoal. The person who gets the charcoal is believed to have **an evil heart**.

On 1st April in France, people eat **chocolate fish** as a treat, and a person who falls for a trick isn't called an April Fool, they are called a **'Poisson d'Avril'** or an 'April fish'.

In America, people used to **pour chocolate** over pieces of cotton on 1st April, to fool their friends with **'cotton candy'**.

The day before Lent is called **Pancake Day** or **Shrove Tuesday** in the UK, **Fat Tuesday** in Brazil, and **Mardi Gras** in France. **Pancakes** are eaten on this day because it is the last day to enjoy fat, butter and eggs, which used to be forbidden during Lent.

At Easter, it's traditional to eat warm **hot cross buns** on Good Friday. The pastry cross on top of the buns symbolises the cross that Jesus died on.

At Christmas, people in the UK eat **19,000 tonnes of turkey**, **120,000 tonnes of potatoes**, **1,200 tonnes of parsnips**, **1,600 tonnes of chestnuts**, **7.5 million carrots**, **16 million packets of stuffing**, **11 million Christmas cakes**, and **40,000 tonnes of clementines**, **mandarins** and **satsumas**.

**Sprouts** were first eaten at Christmas in the Sixteenth Century – and they've been popular ever since!

**175 million mince pies** are eaten in the UK over Christmas. If these were stacked on top of each other, they would stretch **3,262 miles high** – that's nearly **600 times the height of Mount Everest!**

Mince pies get their name from their original filling which contained **minced meat** as well as fruits and spices.

Not everyone eats turkey for Christmas dinner. In Denmark, it's traditional to eat **goose**, in Greece they eat **lamb**, and in Hungary, they eat **spicy chicken**.

In New Zealand and Australia, it's hot in December, and Christmas lunch can be a **picnic** on the beach.

# STRANGE
# BUT TRUE

In some parts of Asia, it's considered **good manners to burp** after a meal, because it shows you've enjoyed the food.

**Pie eating contests** are held every year in America. The winner is the person who gobbles down the most pies in the shortest amount of time.

**Now THAT's my kind of contest.**

In September 2010 at the MTV Video Music Awards in Los Angeles, pop singer Lady Gaga wore **a dress made from meat** that weighed about 30 kilograms.

In the 1830s, **tomato ketchup** was sold as a medicine in the USA to cure any illness. It was called **Dr Miles's Compound Extract of Tomato**.

Foods like beans, sprouts and cabbage **make you fart** because they contain a sugar called raffinose that the body can't use.

In a can of fizzy drink, there are **seven and a half teaspoons** of sugar. If you put a tooth in a glass of this drink overnight, the sugar in the drink would make the tooth go **black**.

Take a small piece of peeled potato and a small piece of peeled apple, close your eyes, hold your nose and eat each piece – you can't tell the difference because without your senses of sight and smell, **they both taste the same**.

It only takes ten minutes to hardboil a hen's egg, but it could take up to four hours if you wanted to hardboil an **ostrich egg**.

In France, people eat approximately **500,000,000 snails** per year.

In 2011, a Dutch farmer invented a new kind of ice cream – **camel flavour** – made from the milk of his herd of camels.

Japan boasts some even weirder ice cream flavours. Would you fancy Basashi ice cream made from **raw horse meat? Octopus** or **whale ice cream?** Or the strange-looking **black ice cream** flavoured with squid ink?

When a well-known crisp company ran a competition for a new and exciting flavour, the winner was **Builder's Breakfast** – sausage, bacon, egg and tomato. The runners up were **Onion Bhaji**, **Fish and Chips**, **Hoisin Duck**, **Cajun Squirrel** (flavoured with spices but not with squirrel!) and **Chilli Chocolate**.

# Bye!

# HORRID HENRY BOOKS

*Horrid Henry*
*Horrid Henry and the Secret Club*
*Horrid Henry Tricks the Tooth Fairy*
*Horrid Henry's Nits*
*Horrid Henry Gets Rich Quick*
*Horrid Henry's Haunted House*
*Horrid Henry and the Mummy's Curse*
*Horrid Henry's Revenge*
*Horrid Henry and the Bogey Babysitter*
*Horrid Henry's Stinkbomb*
*Horrid Henry's Underpants*
*Horrid Henry Meets the Queen*
*Horrid Henry and the Mega-Mean Time Machine*
*Horrid Henry and the Football Fiend*
*Horrid Henry's Christmas Cracker*
*Horrid Henry and the Abominable Snowman*
*Horrid Henry Robs the Bank*
*Horrid Henry Wakes the Dead*
*Horrid Henry Rocks*
*Horrid Henry and the Zombie Vampire*
*Horrid Henry's Monster Movie*

## Early Readers

*Don't Be Horrid, Henry!*
*Horrid Henry's Birthday Party*
*Horrid Henry's Holiday*
*Horrid Henry's Underpants*
*Horrid Henry Gets Rich Quick*
*Horrid Henry and the Football Fiend*
*Horrid Henry's Nits*
*Horrid Henry and Moody Margaret*
*Horrid Henry's Thank You Letter*
*Horrid Henry Reads a Book*
*Horrid Henry's Car Journey*
*Moody Margaret's School*
*Horrid Henry Tricks and Treats*

*Horrid Henry's Christmas Play*
*Horrid Henry's Rainy Day*
*Horrid Henry's Author Visit*
*Horrid Henry's Sports Day*

## Colour Books

*Horrid Henry's Big Bad Book*
*Horrid Henry's Wicked Ways*
*Horrid Henry's Evil Enemies*
*Horrid Henry Rules the World*
*Horrid Henry's House of Horrors*
*Horrid Henry's Dreadful Deeds*
*Horrid Henry Shows Who's Boss*
*Horrid Henry's A-Z of Everything Horrid*

## Joke Books

*Horrid Henry's Joke Book*
*Horrid Henry's Jolly Joke Book*
*Horrid Henry's Might Joke Book*
*Horrid Henry versus Moody Margaret*
*Horrid Henry's Hilariously Horrid Joke Book*
*Horrid Henry's Purple Hand Gang Joke Book*
*Horrid Henry's All Time Favourite Joke Book*

## Activity Books

*Horrid Henry's Brainbusters*
*Horrid Henry's Headscratchers*
*Horrid Henry's Mindbenders*
*Horrid Henry's Colouring Book*
*Horrid Henry's Puzzle Book*
*Horrid Henry's Sticker Book*
*Horrid Henry's Classroom Chaos*
*Horrid Henry's Holiday Havoc*
*Horrid Henry Runs Riot*
*Horrid Henry's Annual 2012*

Visit Horrid Henry's website at www.horridhenry.co.uk for
competitions, games, downloads and a monthly newsletter.